Baby Love

allison jane smith

plaids & prints

My Baby Love

There is nothing more special than welcoming a new baby into the world. What better way for a new mother to prepare for the arrival of her baby, than making a beautiful quilt. Baby quilts are an amazing way of creating an heirloom that your child will treasure forever. The projects included in this book range from simple baby gear projects to beautiful quilts. Make something special for your little one today!

Dedication

For my three baby loves,
Belle Emmaline
Dylan Everett
Felicity Jane
And the love of my life, Mike.

Acknowledgement

Jim Yost, *Yost Photography*
www.yostphotograpy.com
Sarah Milne, *Daffodil Design*
www.daffodildesign.com

www.plaidsandprints.com

ISBN 0-9770864-4-5

Copyright © 2008 Reproduction of any part of this book without written consent from Plaids and Prints is prohibited under United States Copyright Law. The information in this book is presented in good faith, but no warranty is given nor results guaranteed. Since Plaids and Prints has no control over choice of materials or procedures, the company assumes no responsibility for the use of this information.

Table of Contents

- Beginner's Basics 4
- Perfect Piecing 5
- Finishing Your Quilt 6
- Sugar Coated 8
- Memory Monogram 10
- First Flutter 12
- First Flight 15
- Pear on Houndstooth 18
- Set Sail 21
- Rosebuds 24
- Little Man 27
- Fuzzy Wuzzy 34
- Fuzzy Wuzzy, Take 2 36
- Little Miss Ruffle 38
- Butterfly Onesie 40
- Burp Cloths 43
- Diaper Pouch 44
- Polka Dot Blanket 46
- Hooded Towel 49
- Glossary 54

Beginner's Basics

FABRIC

Purchase 100% cotton high-quality fabric. These fabrics are easier to work with, and will hold up better over time. The measurements in this book are based on 44" wide fabric, unless otherwise stated.

High quality fabric does not need to be prewashed. The fabric should not bleed, and as long as 100% cotton is used throughout the quilt, the shrinkage should be uniform. If prewashing is more comfortable, go right ahead.

THREADS

Use 100% cotton thread for piecing and quilting. Match the thread color with the colors in the quilt. If the quilt has many colors, choose a neutral, such as cream, gray or white.

NEEDLES

The best needles for machine piecing, quilting and binding quilts with 100% cotton fabrics are 75/11 or 80/12. It is a good idea to change your needle after every long project.

ROTARY-CUTTING

Although there are a variety of rotary cutters available, a great size to start with is the 45mm. The cutters with the retractable blades are a great choice. It is important to make sure you always have a sharp blade.

In order for your rotary cutting to be effective, you will need a clear, acrylic ruler. The 6" x 24", with $1/4$" grid, is the best choice for your first ruler.

Another essential tool for rotary cutting is a self-healing rotary mat. The smallest mat you should buy is a 17" x 23" mat, marked with a 1" grid. You should always use your clear, acrylic ruler for the most precise measuring.

SEWING MACHINE

As long as your machine has a good straight stitch, with good tension, you will be able to make a quilt. A good investment for any quilter is a $1/4$" foot, which does not normally come with sewing machines.

IRON AND IRONING BOARD

Place a clean iron and ironing board close to your sewing workstation. It is most effective when you use steam while pressing.

Perfect Piecing

SEAMS

When using your ¼" foot on your sewing machine, the edge of the fabric should run along the edge of the presser foot while piecing.

Set your sewing machine to a stitch length of 10 to 12 stitches per inch, which is equivalent to a 2.0 - 2.5 mm setting.

PINNING

To line up the seams on the patchwork pieces perfectly, pin the pieces together first.

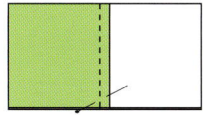

When piecing rows together, it is helpful to pin where the seams line up in opposite direction, in order to make sure the blocks abut when they are sewn together.

PRESSING

For accurate patchwork, press as you sew. Press the seam flat to set the stitches, then use your iron to press to one side. Do not press the seams open.

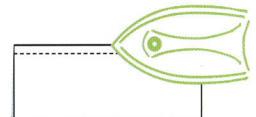 

Applique

Follow the manufacturer's instructions for your fusible web. Light to medium weight fusible web will give the best results. All of the templates have been reversed for easy tracing. Trace applique shapes onto the back of the fusible web with a pencil. Cut approximately ¼" around each shape. Iron the fusible web onto the wrong side of the fabric. Cut out the shape exactly on the traced lines. Peel the paper backing, position the shape and when you are satisfied with the arrangement, press, overlapping pieces as necessary. Finish the edges with a machine button hole stitch in a neutral thread. You can do this as you are doing the applique, or while you are quilting to save time. If you would like to applique using the traditional method, go ahead, just make the ¼" adjustment.

Signing your Quilt

Before your quilt is finished, it needs to be signed. You should include your name, the name of the quilt, and the date. If your quilt was made as a gift also include the recipient, relationship, and occasion.

Finishing Your Quilt

BATTING

Although there are many choices when it comes to batting, 80/20 cotton-polyester batting gives a nice, clean result. This type of batting is easy to machine quilt and lies flat when finished. The package the batting comes in should tell you the maximum distance recommended between the lines of quilting.

LAYERING YOUR QUILT

Cut the backing and batting 6" larger than the quilt top. Lay the backing, right side down, on a large work table or floor. Secure the edges with masking tape. Center the batting and the quilt top, right side up, on the backing and smooth out any wrinkles. Beginning in the center, baste the quilt with safety pins. Place pins every 3" to 4".

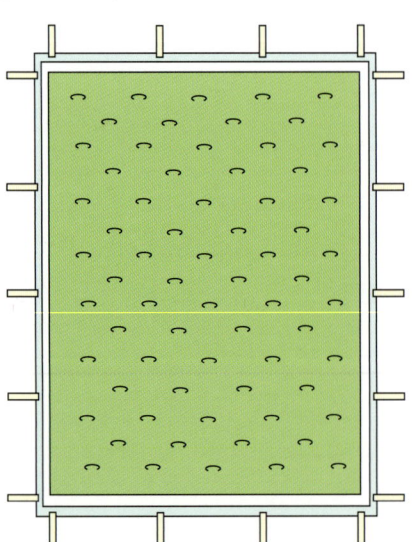

MACHINE QUILTING

For best results, use a walking foot for straight lines and a darning foot for free-motion quilting. Begin by bringing the bobbin thread up to the top of the quilt.

Make a few stitches with the stitch length set at 0. This will secure the quilting stitches. Reset the stitch length to your normal setting and continue stitching.

For stippling or free-motion quilting, disengage the feed dogs on your machine. Guide the quilt under the needle with both hands, working at an even pace so the stitches will be consistent in length.

Stippling

To end a line of quilting, return the stitch length to 0 and stitch. Cut the thread on the top and bottom of the quilt.

When finished quilting, use your rotary-cutting equipment to trim excess batting and backing even with the quilt top.

BINDING

Cut the binding strips at 2½" width. Each of the patterns in this book will specify how many strips you will need. With right sides together, place one strip perpendicular to the other as shown. Stitch. Trim the excess fabric and press.

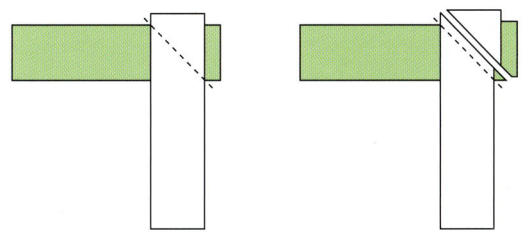

Fold the strip in half lengthwise, wrong sides together, and press. Cut one end of the strip at a 45° angle and turn under ¼". Press. This will be the beginning of the binding.

Starting on one side of the quilt, leaving a 3" tail, sew the binding to the quilt. Keep the raw edges of the binding even with the quilt top edge. End the stitching ¼" from the corner of the quilt and raise the needle.

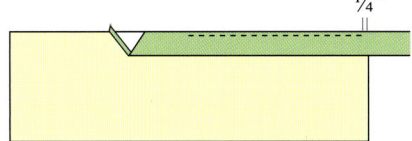

Lift the presser foot. Turn the quilt so the machine will be stitching down the next side. Fold the fabric up away from the quilt.

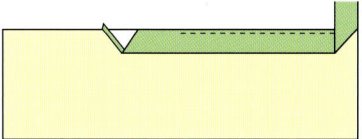

Fold the binding down, parallel with the edge of the quilt top. Start stitching ¼" from the edge. Repeat for remaining corners.

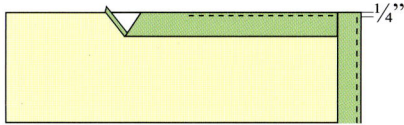

When the beginning is reached, overlap the stitches about 1" and trim the excess binding at a 45° angle. Tuck the end of the binding in the fold and finish the seam.

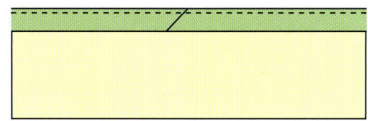

Fold the binding to the back, making sure to cover the stitches. Blindstitch. Tuck the corners to form miters.

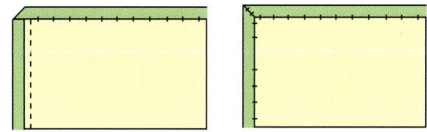

Sugar Coated

30" x 40"

Sweet.
This quilt would sweeten up any nursery. Throwing some greens and blues into a pink and brown quilt gives it some depth. I used my *Charm Bracelet* fabrics in this quilt. Ask for them at your favorite quilt store.

MATERIALS
½ yard of a white print
¼ yard each of eight prints
⅜ yard of a light pink print for binding
1¼ yards of a backing fabric
34" x 44" piece of batting
fusible web
2 yards of a ribbon
1 yard each of two ribbons

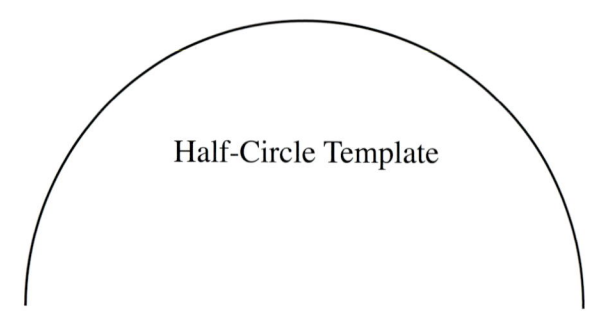

Half-Circle Template

CUT

From the white print, cut:
- 2 - 4½" x 30½" strips
- 1 - 2½" x 30½" strips

From the other prints, cut a total of:
- 1 - 5½" x 30½" strips
- 5 - 4½" x 30½" strips
- 3 - 3½" x 30½" strips
- 2 - 2½" x 30½" strips

From the ribbons, cut a total of:
- 2 - 30½" matching strips
- 2 - 30½" strips

From the light pink binding strip, cut:
- 4 - 2½" x 42" binding strips

PREPARE

Cut two 4" x 30" strips of fusible web. Draw a line 1½" in along the long edge. Using the half-circle template provided, trace 10 scallops along the line.

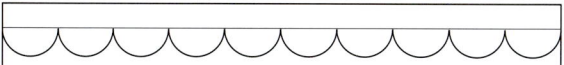

Press the scallops onto the wrong side of two of the 4½" x 30½" strips of fabric. Cut the scallop strips out exactly along the traced scallops. Remove the paper backing. Place the scallop strips onto the two white 4½" x 30½" strips with edges aligned. Press them in place. Sew around the half-circles with a straight stitch, using clear thread.

THE QUILT

Layout the twelve strips, following the diagram below. When you are satisfied with the arrangement, sew the strips together.

Place your ribbon along the strips, as shown on the diagram below. Pin in place. When you are satisfied with the arrangement, sew down the center of the length of the ribbon using coordinating thread.

FINISHING

Layer the quilt top, batting, and backing. Pin the layers together. Quilt as desired.

Use the light pink print 2½" x 42" strips to bind the quilt.

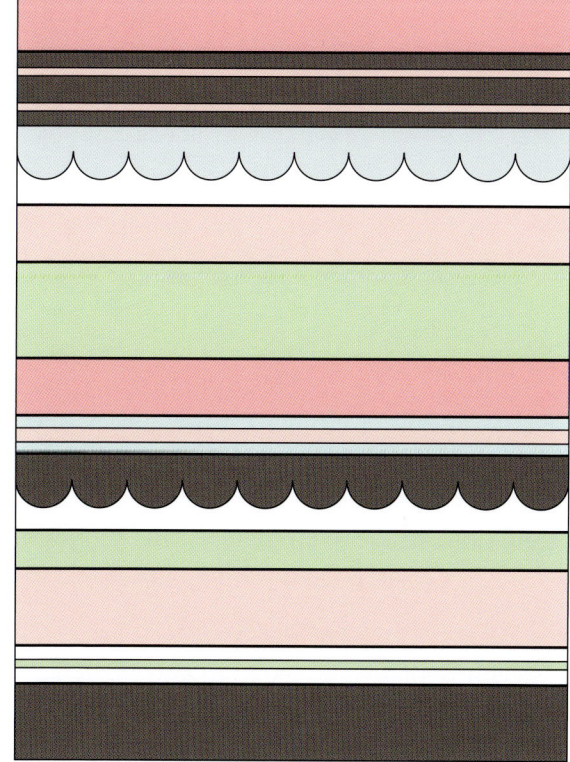

Memory Monogram

28" x 36"

This quilt is the reinvention of the classic t-shirt quilt.
Use your baby's clothes for the fabrics in this quilt. You can create the quilt with the items that were special, or you can choose a specific theme. I used my son's church shirts for this quilt. For baby girls it is fun to include the ruffles and bows that are often found on their clothes.
I did not include a template for the monogram, because I think it is fun to have it be out of your own handwriting. Or, you can choose a favorite font on the computer.

MATERIALS
anything that was special to your baby and you, best if you use washable, cotton fabrics
3/8 yard of a print for binding
1 yard of a backing fabric
32" x 40" piece of batting
fusible web

CUT

From the fabrics, cut a total of:
   59 - 4½" squares
   1 - 8½" square

From the binding fabric, cut:
   4 - 2½" x 42" binding strips

THE QUILT

Lay out the fifty-nine 4½" squares and one 8½" square, referring to the diagram below. Once you are satisfied with the arrangement, sew the blocks together in each row. Press.

Sew the rows together to complete the quilt top. Press. The quilt top should measure 28½" x 36½".

Trace a 9½" square and your letter template onto fusible web. Cut around each shape approximately ¼". Press onto the wrong side of the fabrics. Cut the shapes exactly along the traced lines. Draw a 8¼" square in the center of the 9½" square. Cut along the traced line. Remove the paper backing. Place the square around the outside of the large square, as shown in the diagram below. Press in place. Place the letter centered in the large square. Press in place. Sew around each shape with a straight stitch, using clear thread.

FINISHING

Layer the quilt top, batting, and backing. Pin the layers together. Quilt as desired. Use the 2½" x 42" strips to bind the quilt.

First Flutter

27" x 27"

The oversized wool butterfly applique gives this simple quilt a touch of whimsy.
The soft, pastel stripes in this quilt are sweet, but still gives the quilt a fresh, modern touch.
Wrap up your special baby girl in this quilt today!
Also an excellent baby shower gift...

MATERIALS

9 fat quarters of various pastel striped fabrics
1/4 yard of a green print for binding
8" x 11" piece of pink wool
1 yard of a backing fabric
31" x 31" piece of batting
yellow perle cotton

CUT

From each of the striped fat quarters, cut:
 9 - $3\frac{1}{2}$" squares

From the green print, cut:
 3 - $2\frac{1}{2}$" x 42" binding strips

THE QUILT

Lay out the eighty-one $3\frac{1}{2}$" squares, nine across and nine down, referring to the diagram below. Once you are satisfied with the arrangement, sew the blocks together in each row. Press.

Sew the rows together to complete the quilt top. Press. The quilt top should measure $27\frac{1}{2}$" x $27\frac{1}{2}$".

FINISHING

Layer the quilt top, batting, and backing. Pin the layers together. Quilt as desired.

Use the green print $2\frac{1}{2}$" x 42" strips to bind the quilt.

Trace the butterfly template onto the dark pink wool. Cut out the butterfly along the traced edges. Place the butterfly onto the quilt top in the desired location, following the diagram below. Pin in place. Using perle cotton, appliqué the butterfly to the quilt using a blanket stitch.

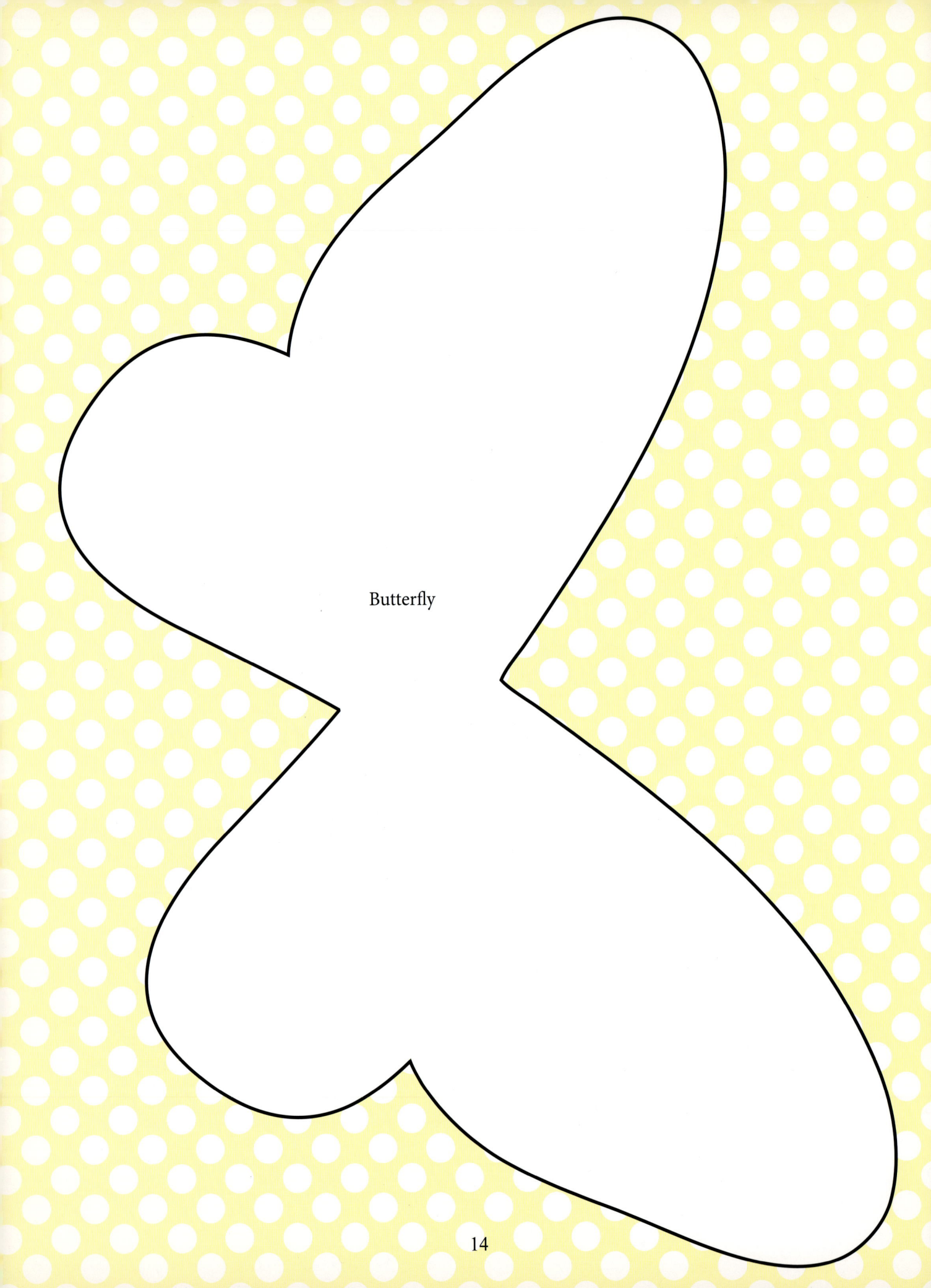
Butterfly

First Flight

30" x 30"

This adorable little quilt is perfect for cuddling and playing while on-the-go. It is a simple quilt, with an added touch of a wool airplane to make it special. Sometimes it is difficult to find quilting fabrics for boys quilts. If you are having trouble locating anything without a floral print, plaids and stripes are a fun alternative.

MATERIALS

10 fat quarters of various striped fabrics
3/8 yard of a red plaid for binding
9" square of brown wool
1 yard of a backing fabric
34" x 34" piece of batting
red perle cotton

CUT

From the striped fat quarters, cut a total of:
    75 - 2½" x 6½" rectangles

From the red plaid, cut:
    4 - 2½" x 42" binding strips

THE QUILT

Lay out the seventy-five 2½" x 6½" rectangles, fifteen across and five down, referring to the diagram below. Once you are satisfied with the arrangement, sew the blocks together in each row. Press.

Sew the rows together to complete the quilt top. Press. The quilt top should measure 30½" x 30½".

FINISHING

Layer the quilt top, batting, and backing. Pin the layers together. Quilt as desired.

Use the red plaid 2½" x 42" strips to bind the quilt.

Trace the airplane template onto the brown wool. Cut out the airplane along the traced edges. Place the airplane onto the quilt top in the desired location, following the diagram below. Pin in place. Using perle cotton, appliqué the airplane to the quilt using a blanket stitch.

Airplane

Pear on Houndstooth

32" x 32"

What a perfect quilt for a modern nursery.
The houndstooth background brings a classic pattern, and then a pear is appliquéed on for a fresh, unexpected addition. A neutral color palette makes it perfect for a little boy or girl!
After quilting, I added a few touches to the pear with some perle cotton.

MATERIALS

5/8 yard of a yellow print
5/8 yard of a blue print
1/2 yard of a green print for binding and pear
5" square of a light green print for pear center
1 yard of a backing fabric
36" x 36" piece of batting
fusible web

CUT

From the yellow print, cut:

64 - 2½" x 4½" rectangles

From blue print, cut:

64 - 2½" x 4½" rectangles

From the green print, cut:

4 - 2½" x 42" binding strips

THE BLOCK

To make the houndstooth block, sew one yellow 2½" x 4½" rectangle on one blue 2½" x 4½" rectangle, as shown. Make 64.

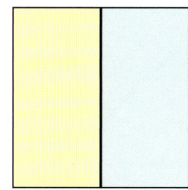

Layout four pieced squares, as shown below, to complete the block. Make 16.

THE QUILT

Lay out the sixteen blocks, four across and four down, referring to the diagram.

Sew the blocks together in each row. Press. Sew the rows together to complete the quilt top. Press. The quilt top should measure 32½" x 32½".

Trace one pear, one leaf, one center, and three seeds on fusible web. Cut around each shape approximately ¼". Press the center onto the wrong side of the light green fabric. Press the rest of the shapes onto the wrong side of the green fabric. Cut the shapes out exactly along the traced lines.

Remove the paper backing. Layer the pear onto the quilt top in the desired location, following the diagram below. When you are satisfied with the arrangement, press it in place. Sew around each shape with a straight stitch, using clear thread.

FINISHING

Layer the quilt top, batting, and backing. Pin the layers together. Quilt as desired. Use the green print 2½" x 42" strips to bind the quilt.

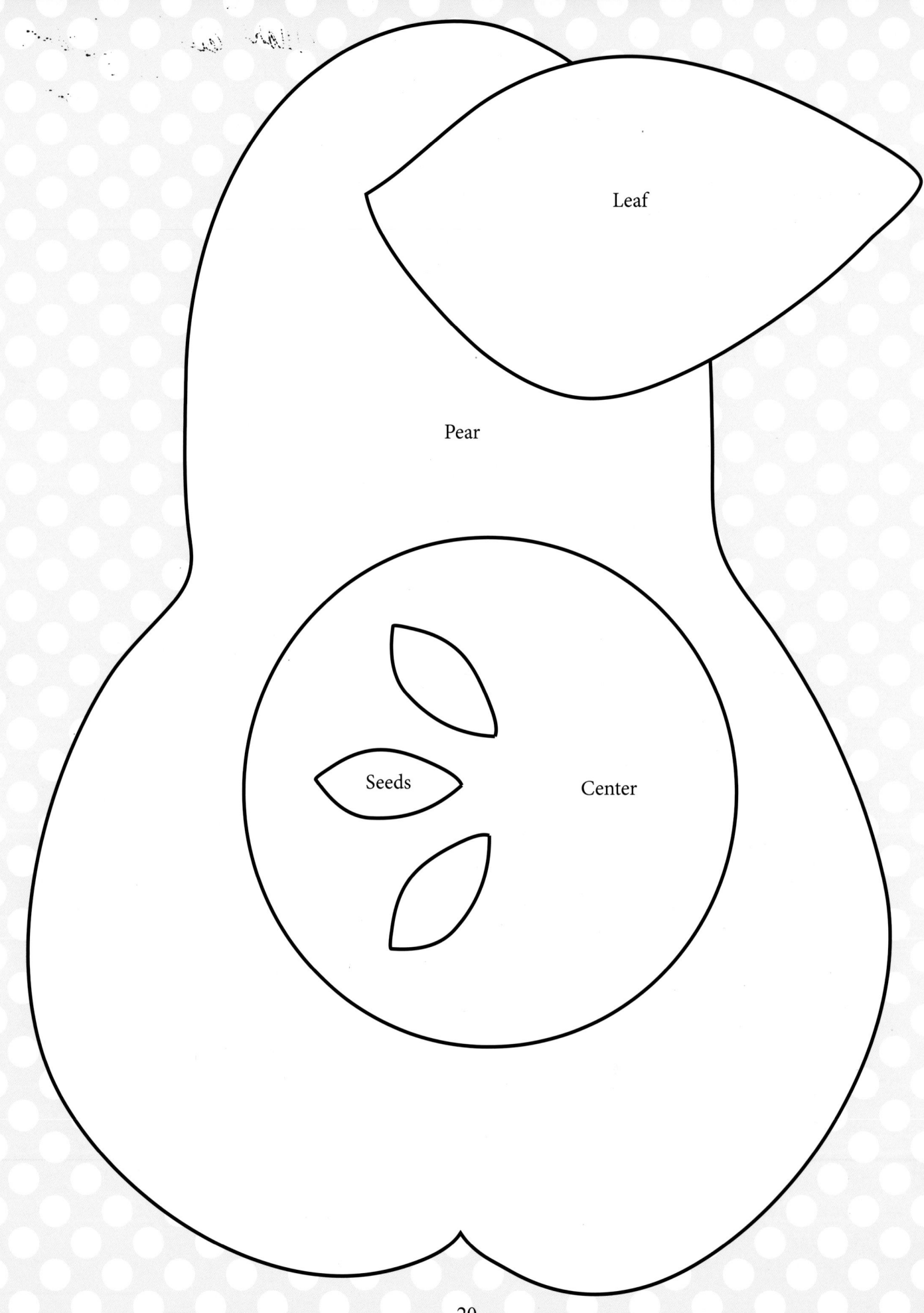

Mary's Quilt — 41" (+6" drop) x 57"

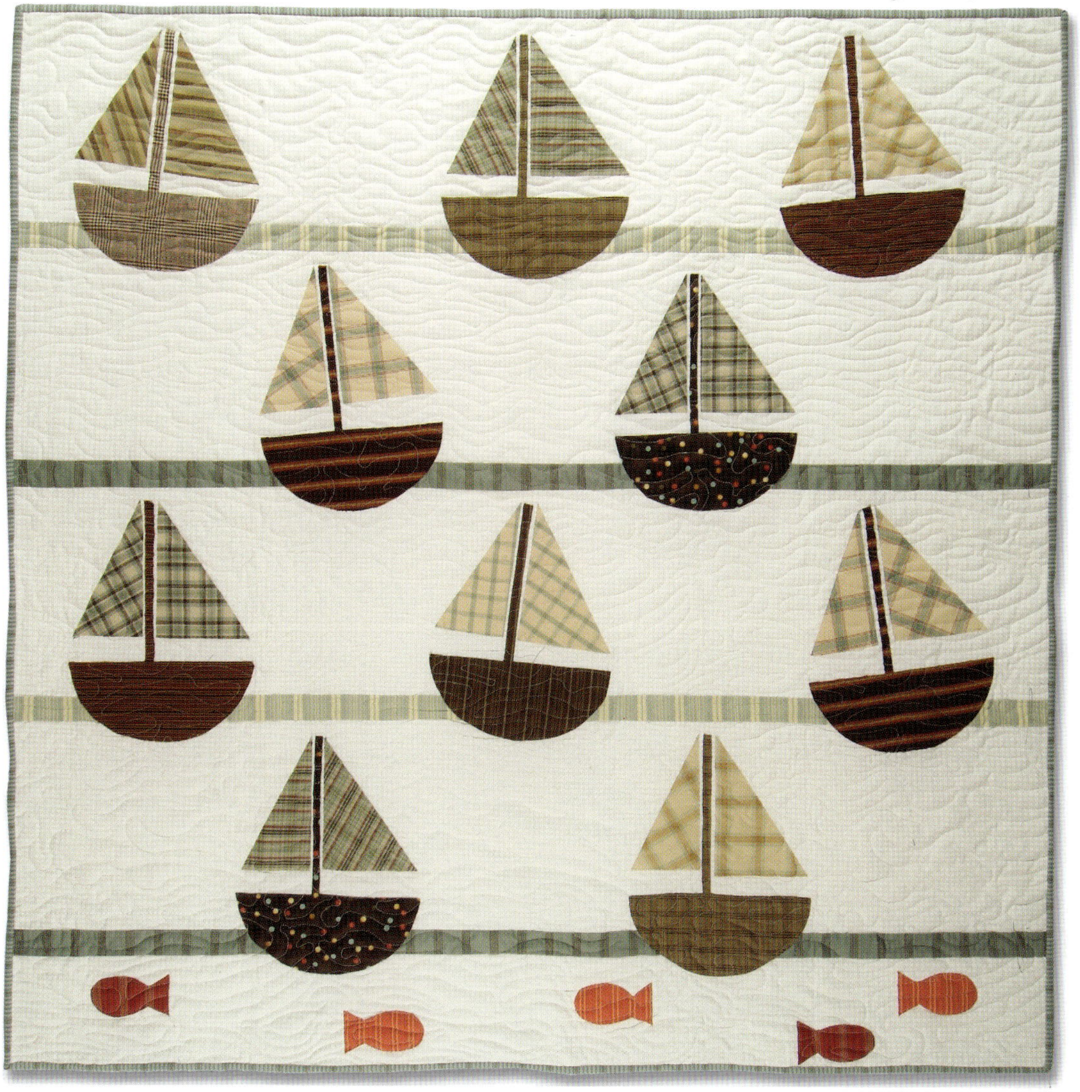

Set Sail

40" x 40"

This nautical quilt is a fun way to bring an adventurous feeling into your nursery. After all, this special time is the beginning of your adventure together.

MATERIALS

1 1/8 yards of a white print
1/4 yard each of two blue stripes
5 fat quarters of brown plaids for boats
5 fat quarters of light blue plaids for sails
6" square each of a red and orange fabric
3/8 yard of a blue stripe for binding
1 1/4 yard of a backing fabric
44" x 44" piece of batting
fusible web

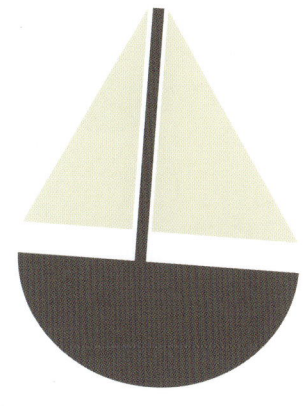

CUT

From the white print, cut:
- 4 - 8½" x 40½" strips
- 1 - 4½" x 40½" strip

From the two blue prints, cut a total of:
- 4 - 1½" x 40½" strips

From the blue binding strip, cut:
- 5 - 2½" x 42" binding strips

THE QUILT

Lay out the white and blue strips, referring to the diagram below. Sew the strips together. Press. The quilt top should measure 40½" x 40½".

Trace ten boats, ten sail sets and five fish on fusible web. Cut around each shape approximately ¼".

Press the boats onto the wrong side of the brown fabrics, the sails onto the wrong side of the light blue fabrics, and the fish onto the wrong side of the red and orange fabrics. Cut the shapes out exactly along the traced lines.

Remove the paper backing. Place the shapes onto the quilt top in the desired location, referring to the diagram below. When you are satisfied with the arrangement, press them in place. Sew around each shape with a straight stitch, using clear thread.

FINISHING

Layer the quilt top, batting, and backing. Pin the layers together. Quilt as desired.

Use the blue print 2½" x 42" strips to bind the quilt.

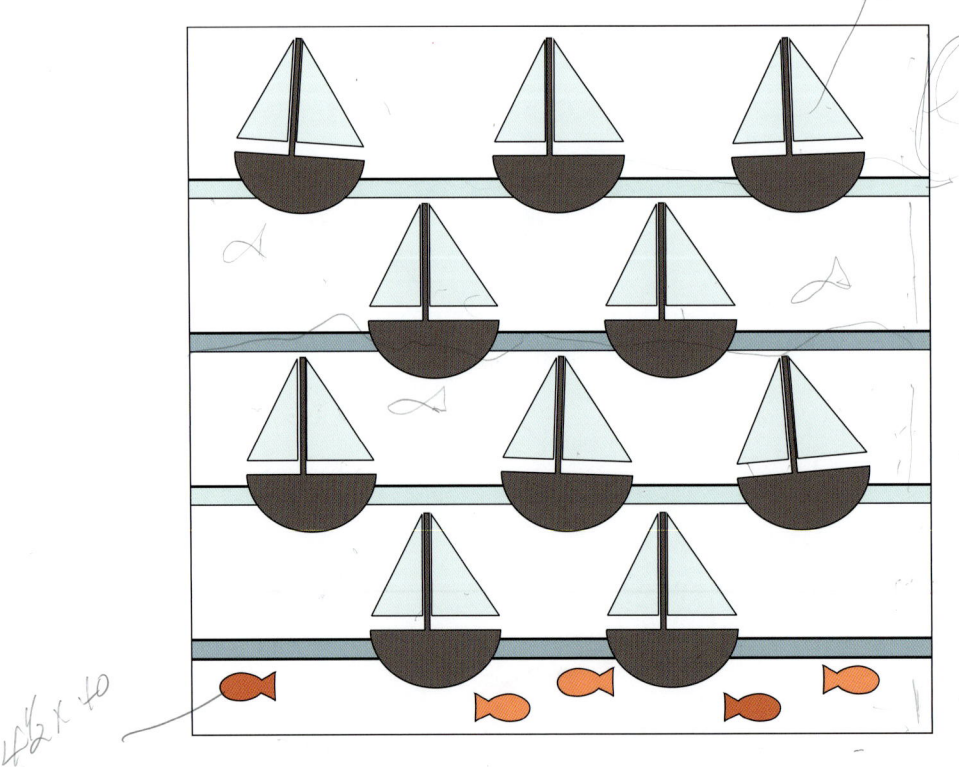

Rosebuds

40" x 40"

This is a perfect baby quilt! As simple as it is cute. The graphic floral design will add a modern twist to any nursery. This quilt is easy enough for a beginner. Simple is adorable!

MATERIALS
1¼ yards of a white print
¼ yard of three green prints
⅛ yard of a dark pink print for the rosebuds
⅛ yard of a pink print for rosebud centers
⅜ yard of a green print for binding
1¼ yards of a backing fabric
44" x 44" piece of batting
fusible web

CUT

From the white print, cut:
  2 - 6½" x 40½" strips
  3 - 8½" x 40½" strips

From the three green prints, cut a total of:
  4 - 1½" x 40½" strips

From the green binding strip, cut:
  5 - 2½" x 42" binding strips

THE QUILT

Lay out the white and green strips, referring to the diagram below. Sew the strips together. Press. The quilt top should measure 40½" x 40½".

Trace seven rosebuds, seven centers, and eight sets of leaves on fusible web. Cut around each shape approximately ¼".

Press the rosebuds onto the wrong side of the dark pink fabric, the centers onto the wrong side of the light pink fabric, and the leaves onto the wrong side of the green fabrics. Cut the shapes out exactly along the traced lines.

Remove the paper backing. Place the shapes onto the quilt top in the desired locations, referring to the diagram below. When you are satisfied with the arrangement, press them in place. Sew around each shape with a straight stitch, using clear thread.

FINISHING

Layer the quilt top, batting, and backing. Pin the layers together. Quilt as desired.

Use the green print 2½" x 42" strips to bind the quilt.

25

Little Man

36" x 48"

What will your little man be when he grows up?
This quilt is all about the dreams that we have for our boys, the type of man they will become.
If there is anything special to your family that I did not include, feel free to customize.
Make it perfect for your little man.

MATERIALS
20 fat quarters of various stripes and plaids
$3/8$ yard of orange plaid for binding
$1\frac{1}{2}$ yards of a backing fabric
40" x 52" piece of batting
fusible web

CUT

From each of 12 fat quarters, cut:
- 1 - 8½" squares
- 2 - 2½" x 8½" rectangles
- 2 - 2½" x 12½" rectangles

From the orange plaid, cut:
- 5 - 2½" x 42" binding strips

THE BLOCK

To make the block, lay out two matching 2½" x 8½" rectangles and two matching 2½" x 12½" rectangles, and a 8½" square, as shown.

Sew the side rectangles to the square. Press. Sew the rectangles on the top and bottom. Press. Make 12.

Using the remaining fabric from the fat quarters, follow the instructions for creating the shirt appliques.

Lumberjack Block

Trace one shirt, one collar set and one button strip on fusible web. Cut around each shape approximately ¼". Press onto the wrong side of a plaid fabric. Cut the shapes out exactly along the traced lines. Remove the paper backing. Layer the shirt onto the center of a block. Press in place.

Referee Block

Trace one shirt on fusible web. Cut around the shirt approximately ¼". Press onto the wrong side of a black and white striped fabric. Cut the shirt out exactly along the traced lines. Remove the paper backing. Place the shirt onto the center a block. Press in place.

Lifeguard Block

Trace one tanktop, and one cross on fusible web. Cut around each shape approximately ¼". Press the tanktop onto the wrong side of a light fabric, and the cross onto the wrong side of a red fabric. Cut each shape out exactly along the traced lines. Remove the paper backing. Layer the shirt onto the center of a block. Press in place.

Pocket Tee Block

Trace one shirt and one pocket on fusible web. Cut around each shape approximately ¼". Press onto the wrong side of a light blue fabric. Cut the shapes out exactly along the traced lines. Remove the paper backing. Layer the shirt onto the center of a block. Press in place.

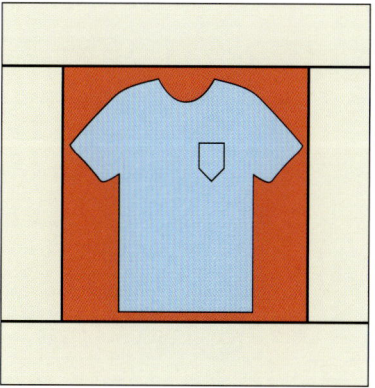

Basketball Jersey Block

Trace one tanktop, and one "17" on fusible web. Cut around each shape approximately ¼". Press the tanktop onto the wrong side of an orange fabric, and the "17" onto the wrong side of a blue fabric. Cut each shape out exactly along the traced lines. Remove the paper backing. Layer the shirt onto the center of a block. Press in place.

Polo Block

Trace one shirt, one collar set and one short button strip on fusible web. Cut around each shape approximately ¼". Press onto the wrong side of a stripe green fabric. Cut the shapes out exactly along the traced lines. Remove the paper backing. Layer the shirt onto the center of a block. Press in place.

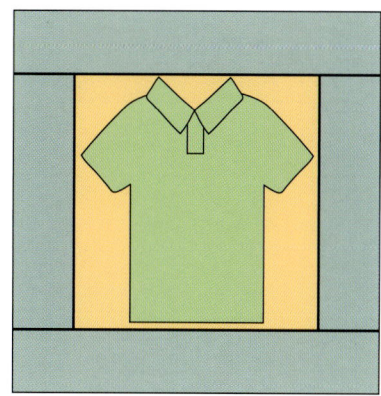

Fireman Block

Trace one shirt, one collar set and one fireman badge on fusible web. Cut around each shape approximately ¼". Press the badge onto the wrong side of a yellow fabric, and the rest on the wrong side of a red fabric. Cut the shapes out exactly along the traced lines. Remove the paper backing. Layer the shirt onto the center of a block. Press in place.

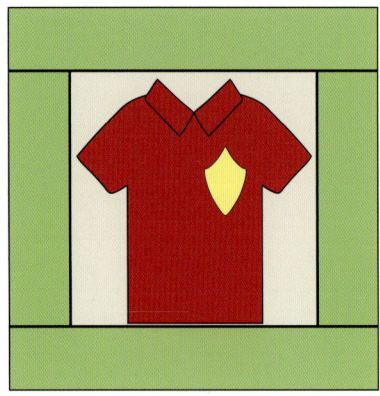

Rugby Jersey Block

Trace one shirt, one sleeve set, and one "2" on fusible web. Cut around each shape approximately ¼". Press the shirt onto the wrong side of an yellow fabric, and the rest onto the wrong side of a green fabric. Cut each shape out exactly along the traced lines. Remove the paper backing. Layer the shirt onto the center of a block. Press in place.

Clown Block

Trace one shirt, one collar set, one button strip, and one bowtie on fusible web. Cut around each shape approximately ¼". Press the bowtie onto the wrong side of an orange fabric, and the rest on the wrong side of a blue fabric. Cut the shapes out exactly along the traced lines. Remove the paper backing. Layer the shirt onto the center of a block. Press in place.

Rockstar Block

Trace one shirt and one star on fusible web. Cut around each shape approximately ¼". Press the shirt onto the wrong side of a brown fabric, and the star on the wrong side of a light blue fabric. Cut the shapes out exactly along the traced lines. Remove the paper backing. Layer the shirt onto the center of a block. Press in place.

Policeman Block

Trace one shirt, one collar set, one button strip, and one policeman badge on fusible web. Cut around each shape approximately ¼". Press the badge onto the wrong side of a yellow fabric, and the rest on the wrong side of a navy blue fabric. Cut the shapes out exactly along the traced lines. Remove the paper backing. Layer the shirt onto the center of a block. Press in place.

Business Man Block

Trace one shirt, one collar set, one button strip, and one tie on fusible web. Cut around each shape approximately ¼". Press the tie onto the wrong side of a striped fabric, and the rest on the wrong side of a light fabric. Cut the shapes out exactly along the traced lines. Remove the paper backing. Layer the shirt onto the center of a block. Press in place.

THE QUILT

Lay out the twelve blocks, three across and four down, referring to the diagram below.

Once you are satisfied with the arrangement, sew the blocks together in each row. Press.

Sew the rows together to complete the quilt top. Press. The quilt top should measure 36½" x 48½".

FINISHING

Layer the quilt top, batting, and backing. Pin the layers together. Quilt as desired.

Use the orange plaid 2½" x 42" strips to bind the quilt.

Fuzzy Wuzzy

40" x 40"

The chenille in this quilt makes it so warm and snugly. It is a perfect place to set your baby to let them play with their toys. Or simply wrap them up in it, and sing them a lullaby. Whatever you do, your baby will love its 'fuzzy wuzzy' warmth.

MATERIALS
16 fat quarters of various shade of 30s fabrics
7 fat quarters of various shades of chenille
$3/8$ yard of a green print for binding
$1 1/4$ yards of a backing fabric
44" x 44" piece of batting

CUT

From each fat quarter, cut:
2 - $2\frac{1}{2}$" x $6\frac{1}{2}$" rectangles
2 - $2\frac{1}{2}$" x $10\frac{1}{2}$" rectangles

From the chenille, cut a total of:
16 - $6\frac{1}{2}$" squares

From the green print, cut:
5 - $2\frac{1}{2}$" x 42" binding strips

THE BLOCKS

To make the block, lay out two matching $2\frac{1}{2}$" x $6\frac{1}{2}$" rectangles, two matching $2\frac{1}{2}$" x $10\frac{1}{2}$" rectangles and a $6\frac{1}{2}$" chenille square, as shown.

Sew the side rectangles to the square. Press. Sew the rectangles onto the top and bottom. Press. Make 16.

THE QUILT

Lay out the sixteen blocks, four across and four down, referring to the diagram below.

Once you are satisfied with the arrangement, sew the blocks together in each row. Press.

Sew the rows together to complete the quilt top. Press. The quilt top should measure $40\frac{1}{2}$" x $40\frac{1}{2}$".

FINISHING

Layer the quilt top, batting, and backing. Pin the layers together. Quilt as desired.

Use the green print $2\frac{1}{2}$" x 42" strips to bind the quilt.

Fuzzy Wuzzy, Take 2

30" x 30"

I made this variation to show what it would look like in primary colors, with all of the blocks using the same color of khaki chenille. It is also smaller than the original, perfect for times when you are on-the-go. This is quite possibly the quilt that will be dragged around the house for years!

MATERIALS
9 fat quarters of various shades of 30's fabrics
3/8 yard of khaki chenille
3/8 yard of a black print for binding
1 yard of a backing fabric
34" x 34" piece of batting

CUT

From each fat quarter, cut:
  2 - $2\frac{1}{2}$" x $6\frac{1}{2}$" rectangles
  2 - $2\frac{1}{2}$" x $10\frac{1}{2}$" rectangles

From the khaki chenille, cut:
  9 - $6\frac{1}{2}$" squares

From the black print, cut:
  4 - $2\frac{1}{2}$" x 42" binding strips

THE BLOCKS

To make the block, lay out two matching $2\frac{1}{2}$" x $6\frac{1}{2}$" rectangles, two matching $2\frac{1}{2}$" x $10\frac{1}{2}$" rectangles and a $6\frac{1}{2}$" chenille square, as shown.

Sew the side rectangles to the square. Press. Sew the rectangles on the top and bottom. Press. Make 9.

THE QUILT

Lay out the nine blocks, three across and three down, referring to the diagram below.

Once you are satisfied with the arrangement, sew the blocks together in each row. Press.

Sew the rows together to complete the quilt top. Press. The quilt top should measure $30\frac{1}{2}$" x $30\frac{1}{2}$".

FINISHING

Layer the quilt top, batting, and backing. Pin the layers together. Quilt as desired.

Use the black print $2\frac{1}{2}$" x 42" strips to bind the quilt.

Little Miss Ruffle

40" x 40"

What could be more precious than this quilt!
The ruffles on this quilt add an extra layer of love that your baby will adore.
Sweeten up your nursery today!
The presser feet needed for this quilt are easily available at any sewing machine store.

MATERIALS
25 fat quarters of assorted pastel fabrics
3/8 yard of a yellow print for binding
1 1/4 yards of a backing fabric
44" x 44" piece of batting
ruffler presser foot
4mm hemmer foot

CUT

From each fat quarter, cut:
- 2 - 2" x 21" strips
- 1 - 8½" square

From the binding fabric, cut:
- 4 - 2½" x 42" binding strips

THE RUFFLE

Using the 4mm Straight Stitch Hemmer Foot, hem the long edges of your 2" strips of fabric.

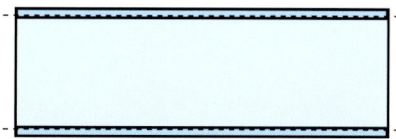

After the edges are hemmed, change your presser foot to the Ruffler foot. Set your presser foot so that it will ruffle after every 6th stitch.

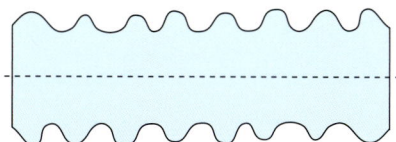

Press the ruffle flat, and trim to 8½" in length. Set aside in matching pairs.

THE BLOCKS

Lay out one 8½" square and two matching ruffle strips, as shown in the diagram below. The ruffle seams should be 2½" from the edge of the square. Sew along the ruffle seam. Make 25.

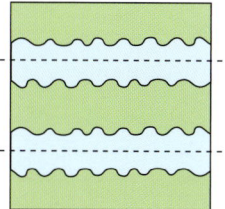

THE QUILT

Lay out the twenty-five blocks, five across and five down, as shown in the diagram below.

Once you are satisfied with the arrangement, sew the blocks together in each row. Press. Sew the rows together to complete the quilt top. Press. The quilt top should measure 40½" x 40½".

FINISHING

Layer the quilt top, batting, and backing. Pin the layers together. Quilt as desired. Use the 2½" x 42" strips to bind the quilt.

Butterfly Onesie

Turn plain into totally adorable.
Nothing could be sweeter for your baby girl!
Just pick up your favorite onesie and add these sweet wings to create a customized look.
It is a simple project that gives big impact.

MATERIALS

1 white onesie
1/4 yard of fabric for wings
8" square of medium weight interfacing

CUT

From the printed fabric, cut:
  2 - 6" x 8" rectangles

From the interfacing, cut:
  1 - 6" x 8" rectangle

THE WINGS

Using the butterfly template, trace the butterfly onto the wrong side of one of the fabric rectangles.

Layer the rectangles, right sides together, with the butterfly tracing facing up. Place the interfacing underneath the fabric rectangles.

Sew along the traced line, leaving a 2" opening, backstitching at the beginning and end.

Cut the butterfly out around the stitched line approximately $1/4$". Turn the butterfly wings right side out. Hand sew the opening closed. Press flat. Top stitch the wings, $1/4$" from the edge.

FINISHING

Place the wings on the back of your onesie, in the desired location. Pin in place. Sew the wings in place, stitching down the middle of the wings.

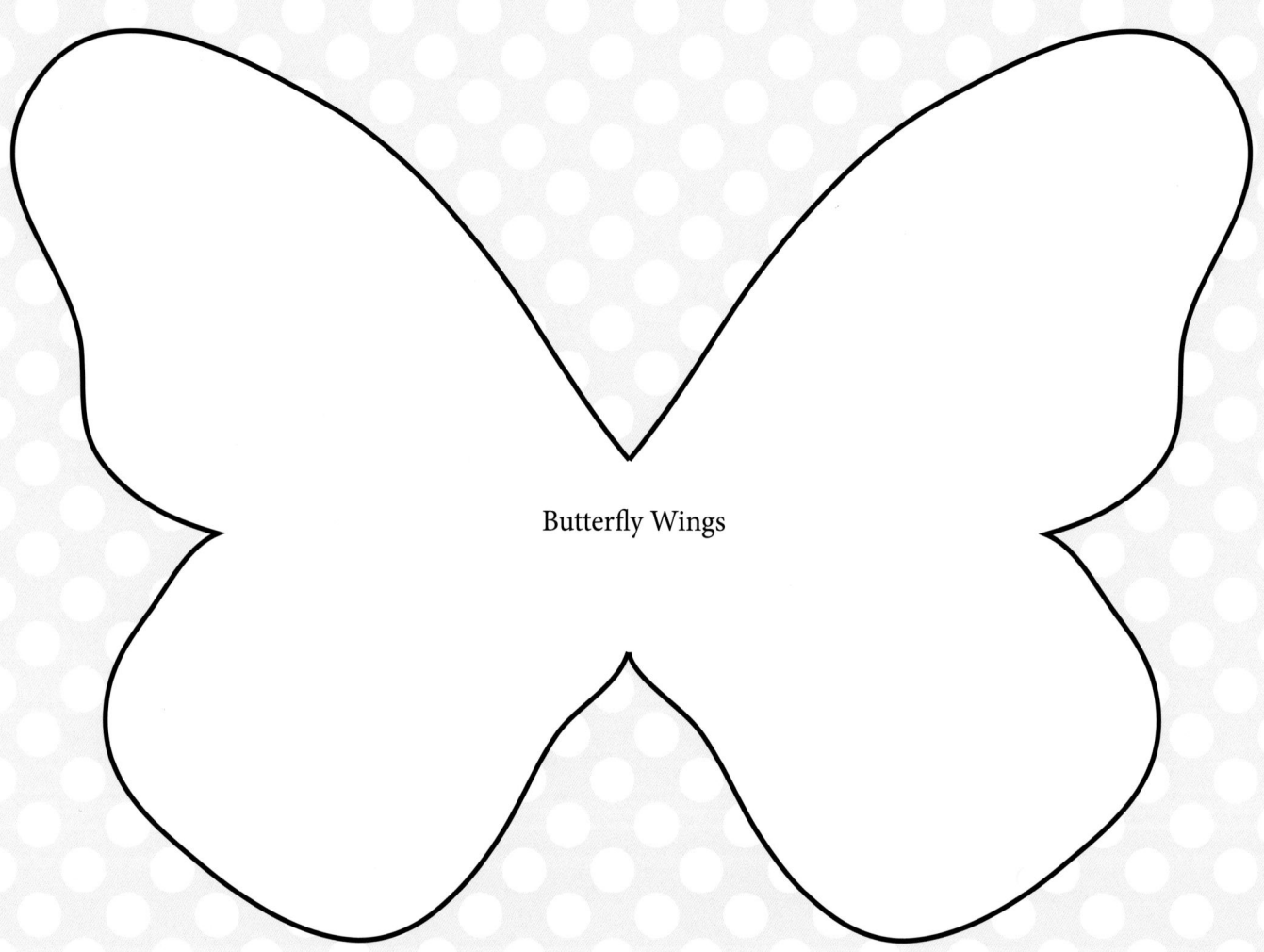

Burp Cloths

Why not make them cute since you have to use them?
Just by adding simple ribbon down the seams of the diaper you have created a stylish burp cloth.
Choose your favorite ribbon. You can match your diaper bag, nursery, or mix them up!

MATERIALS
3½ yards of ribbon
3 cotton reusable diapers

CUT

From the ribbon, cut:
 6 - 21" strips

Lay one of the cotton diapers on a table. Place two of the ribbon strips along the seams of the diaper. Pin in place. Fold the beginning and end of the ribbon under ¼" in order for the ends to have a finished look. Sew along the both edges of the ribbon, using a coordinating thread. Make 3.

Diaper Pouch

Stash your diapers and wipes in this stylish pouch.
I used vinyl fabric coating on the outside of the pouch to make it simple to wipe clean!
It is easy to find at your local craft store.
This pouch is a wonderful accessory for any diaper bag.

MATERIALS
12" x 14" piece of fabric for outside
1/3 yard of fabric for inside
2" x 16" piece of fabric for flower
vinyl fabric coating
button

PREPARE

Cut a 12" x 14" piece of vinyl coating. Iron it onto the right side of your outside fabric.

CUT

From the outside vinyl coated fabric, cut:

    1 - 10" x 12" rectangle

From the inside fabric, cut:

    1 - 10" x 12" rectangle

From the fabric for the flower, cut:

    1 - 1½" x 15" rectangle

THE POUCH

Fold a 10" square in half. Press the fold. Sew ¼" in along the folded edge. Make 2.

Place the 10" x 12" inside fabric rectangle on a table, right side up. Lay the two folded squares on top of the rectangle, as shown below.

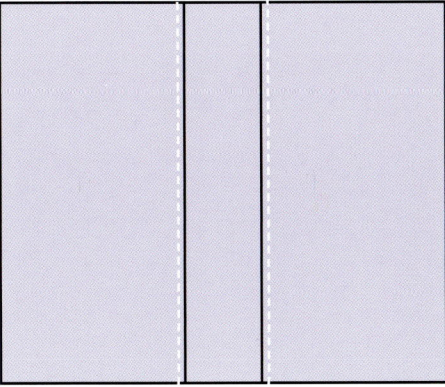

Place the 10" x 12" outside fabric rectangle on top of the other fabric, right side down. Pin well. Sew around the pouch, ¼" in along the edge, leaving a 3" opening, backstitching at the beginning and end.

Turn the pouch right side out. Hand se the opening closed.

FINISHING

Fold the 1½" x 15" rectangle in half, lengthwise. Press. Fold both long raw edges to the center fold. Press. Sew along the center of the strip. Fold the strip into the shape of a flower and tack using perle cotton.

Place onto the pouch in the desired location. When satisfied, sew the center of the flower onto the pouch to secure. Sew a button onto the middle of the flower.

Polka Dot Blanket

26" x 35"

Simple..Cuddly..Polka Dot..Warmth
This blanket will be your baby's favorite. It is so easy to make.
Choose your favorite color and make one today! Or three! They are that easy!
They also make wonderful baby shower gifts.

MATERIALS

1 yard of a 54" colored fleece
¼ yard of a 54" white fleece

CUT

From the colored fleece, cut:
  2 - 26½" x 35½" rectangles

THE BLANKET

Using the circle template, trace 14 circles onto the wrong side of the white fleece. Cut the circles out exactly along the traced lines.

Lay out one of the colored fleece rectangles right side up. Place the white circles in the desire location on the colored fleece. Pin in place.

Sew around the circles on your sewing machine, using straight stitch and white thread.

FINISHING

Layer the two colored fleece rectangles, right sides together. Sew around the outside leaving a 4" opening, backstitching at the beginning and end.

Turn the blanket right side out. Hand stitch the opening closed.

Top stitch the blanket, 1" from the edge, using a straight stitch and thread that matches your fleece.

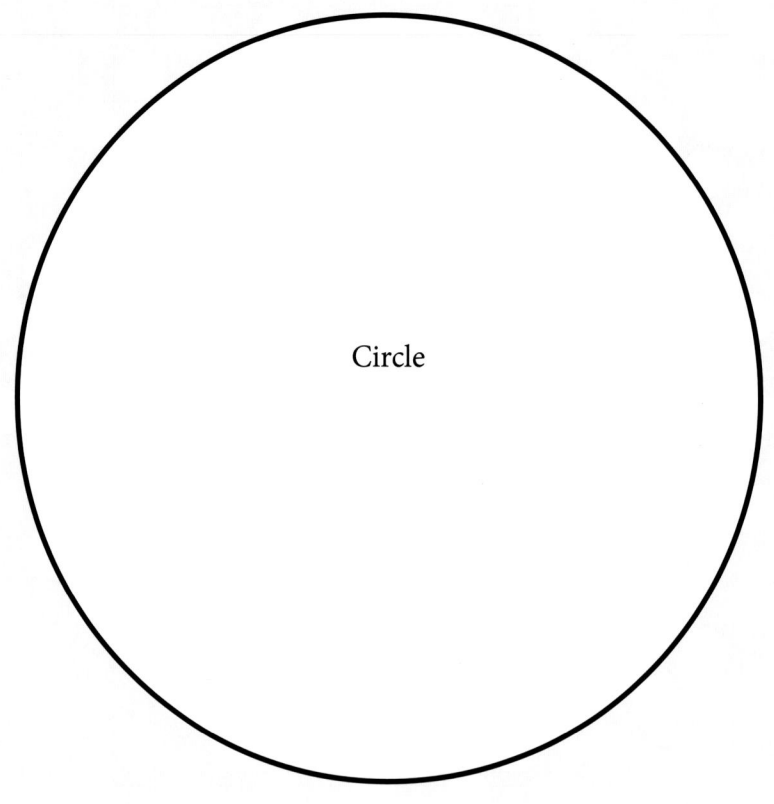

Hooded Towel

Bundle up your baby after bath time in this cozy towel.
The crown on the hood makes this towel special enough for your little prince or princess.
I started with a thick, plush towel to make is as snuggly and warm as possible.

MATERIALS
1 towel larger than 30" x 39"
⅝ yard of fabric for binding
6" square of yellow fabric for crown appliqué
6" square of fusible web

CUT

From the towel, cut:
- 1 - 30" square
- 1 - 10" square, cut diagonally making 2 triangles

From the fabric for the binding, cut:
- 3 - 6" x 42" strips
- 1 - 2 1/2" x 42" strip

THE TOWEL

Trace one crown on fusible web. Cut around the crown approximately 1/4". Press the crown onto the wrong side of the 6" square of yellow fabric. Cut the crown out exactly along the traced lines.

Remove the paper backing. Lay the crown onto the right side of the hood triangle, in the desired location, following the diagram below. When satisfied, press it in place. Stitch around the crown using yellow thread.

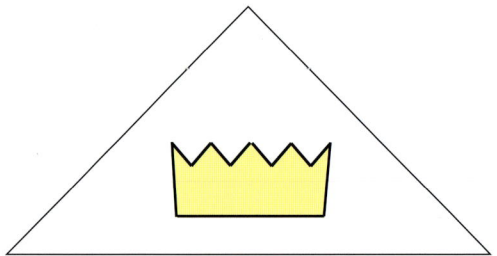

Using the 2½" strip, bind the long edge of the triangle. Pin the triangle to one corner of the 30" square towel.

Bind the layers together and the outside of the 30" square, using the 4½" strips. The binding stitch line should be 1" away from the edge of the towel to create a wide binding.

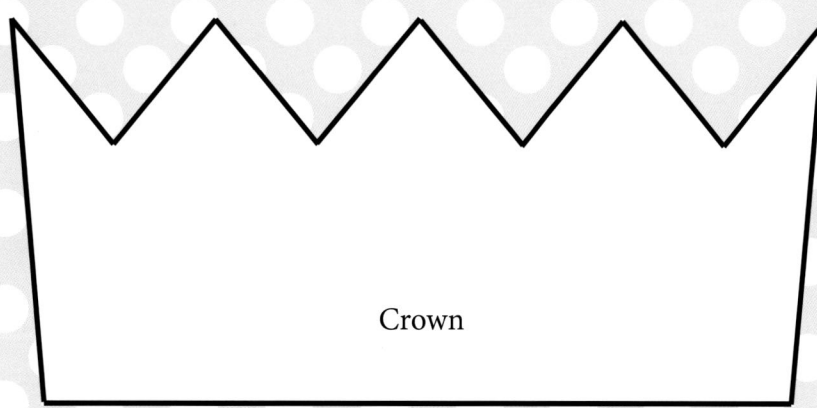
Crown

Other Books From plaids & prints

Long-Arm Quilting

We now offer long-arm quilting services on our Gammill Statler Stitcher. Prices start as low as 1½¢ per square inch, with a minimum charge of $50.00. Contact us to receive specific pricing information for your quilt.
We guarantee a four-week turnaround time.
Take a look at our website to see more information and designs.

www.plaidsandprints.com
info@plaidsandprints.com

Notes

Glossary

BACKING
The fabric that is used for the bottom layer of the quilt.

BACKSTITCH
Short stitches at the beginning and end of a line of stitching. Mainly used on the outer border, binding, and quilting.

BASTE
Loosely securing the layers of the quilt together until it is quilted, either with a large running stitch or safety pins.

BATTING
The layer between the quilt top and backing, which provides the coziness of the quilt.

BIAS
When fabric is cut at a 45° angle, which has the greatest amount of stretch.

BINDING
A narrow strip of fabric used to finish the quilt, by enclosing the raw edges of the quilt top, backing, and batting together.

BLINDSTITCH
Thread the needle with a single strand of thread and tie a knot at the end. To secure the binding, push your needle through the fold of the binding, and just a tiny bit of the backing fabric. Repeat all the way around the quilt.

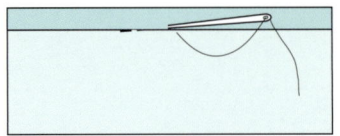

BLOCK
Any design that is usually repeated in the quilt top.

BORDER
The fabric strips surrounding the quilt center, which can be plain or pieced. Not all of the quilts in this book have a border.

FAT QUARTER
An 18" x 22" piece of fabric. Most quilt stores offer pre-cut fat quarters.

MITER
A 45° angle formed in each corner when binding the quilt.

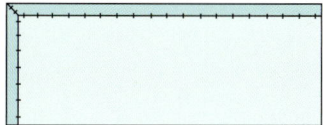

PRESS
To press your seams, do not move the iron while it is on your fabric. Instead, lift the iron off the fabric and place it in another location.

QUILT TOP
The pieced, top layer of the quilt.

QUILTING
The stitching that secures the three layers of the quilt together.

SASHING
The rectangles and strips of fabric that are used to separate blocks.

SEAM
Stitching in order to join two pieces of fabric together, usually with your sewing machine.

SEAM ALLOWANCE
The distance between the raw edge of the fabrics and the stitch line. Always use ¼" seam allowance when making a quilt.

SEW DIAGONALLY
Stitching from and to opposite corners in order to make two triangles.

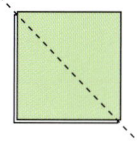 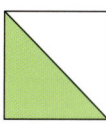

TONE-ON-TONE
Fabric that uses different shades of the same color in the background and print.

Come Visit us on our Blog!
plaidsandprints.blogspot.com

On our Blog, you will find:
Quilting Tutorials
Free Desktop Wallpapers
Free Patterns to Download
Things We Love
Our Latest News